WORLD CULTURES

Zapotecs

SIMON ROSE

www.av2books.com

AV² provides enriched content that supplements and complements this book. Weigl's AV² books strive to create inspired learning and engage young minds in a total learning experience.

Your AV² Media Enhanced books come alive with...

Audio
Listen to sections of the book read aloud.

Key Words
Study vocabulary, and complete a matching word activity.

Video
Watch informative video clips.

Quizzes
Test your knowledge.

Embedded Weblinks
Gain additional information for research.

Slide Show
View images and captions, and prepare a presentation.

Go to www.av2books.com, and enter this book's unique code.

BOOK CODE

W217481

Try This!
Complete activities and hands-on experiments.

... and much, much more!

AV² by Weigl brings you media enhanced books that support active learning.

Published by AV² by Weigl
350 5th Avenue, 59th Floor
New York, NY 10118
Website: www.av2books.com   www.weigl.com

Library of Congress Cataloging-in-Publication Data
Rose, Simon, 1961-
  Zapotecs / Simon Rose.
     pages cm. -- (World cultures)
Includes index.
 Summary: "Facts about the Zapotec indigenous peoples of Mexico. Includes information about their traditions, myths, social activities, the development of their culture, methods of hunting and gathering, rituals, and their daily lives. Intended for fifth to eighth grade students"--Provided by publisher.
  ISBN 978-1-62127-510-7 (hardcover : alk. paper) -- ISBN 978-1-62127-514-5 (softcover : alk. paper)
 1. Zapotec Indians--Mexico--Juvenile literature. I. Title.
 F1221.Z3R67 2014
 972'.00049768--dc23
                        2013000847

Printed in the United States of America in North Mankato, Minnesota
1 2 3 4 5 6 7 8 9 0   17 16 15 14 13

052013
WEP040413

Project Coordinator   Aaron Carr
Art Director   Terry Paulhus

Photo Credits
Every reasonable effort has been made to trace ownership and to obtain permission to reprint copyright material. The publishers would be pleased to have any errors or omissions brought to their attention so that they may be corrected in subsequent printings.

Weigl acknowledges Getty Images as its primary image supplier for this title. Other sources: Alamy: pages 3, 11, 12, 14, 18, 19, 20, 21, 23, and 27. Corbis: page 6. Newscom: page 8. Shutterstock: pages 24 and 25. Wikimedia: page 28.

CONTENTS

Where in the World?

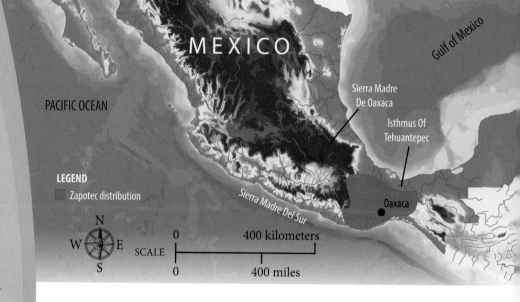

MEXICO

Gulf of Mexico

Sierra Madre De Oaxaca

Isthmus Of Tehuantepec

PACIFIC OCEAN

Sierra Madre Del Sur

Oaxaca

LEGEND
Zapotec distribution

N
W E
S
SCALE

0   400 kilometers

0   400 miles

PACIFIC OCEAN

ATLANTIC OCEAN

MEXICO

SOUTH AMERICA

Population: About
115 million (2011)

Indigenous Population:
About 10 million

Continent: North America

States: There are 31 federal
states in Mexico and one
federal district, where
the capital of Mexico City
is located.

Area: 761,602 square
miles (1,972,550
square kilometers)

The Zapotecs are an **indigenous** people of Mexico. Today, there are four basic groups of Zapotec people living primarily in the southern state of Oaxaca, Mexico. One group, the Southern Zapotecs, live in the southern mountains of the Sierra Madre del Sur. Another group, called the Serranos, makes its home in the northern mountains of the Sierra Madre de Oaxaca. The Valley of Oaxaca is the home of the Central Valley Zapotecs. A group of Zapotecs called the Istmeno live in the southern **Isthmus** of Tehuantepec. Combined, the Zapotecs make up the largest indigenous group in southern Mexico.

Zapotec people have also emigrated from Mexico. Groups of Zapotec communities have made their homes in the United States, especially in the city of Los Angeles and other parts of California. The current population of Zapotec people worldwide is estimated to be between 800,000 and 1,000,000.

Before the arrival of the Spanish conquerors in the early 16th century, the Zapotec civilization was one of the most highly developed cultures in Mesoamerica. Mesoamerica is a region stretching from central Mexico south into parts of present-day Guatemala, Belize, Honduras, El Salvador, and Nicaragua. Mesoamerica was home to a number of ancient civilizations, including the **Aztecs**, **Mayans**, and Zapotecs.

Monte Albán was built on a hill, giving its residents a clear view of the surrounding valley. Today, some Zapotecs consider it a sacred site.

Scientists have found evidence of an advanced Zapotec culture dating back at least 2,500 years.

The ancient city of Monte Albán was the main political and economic center of the Zapotec culture for about 1,000 years. The site has impressive buildings, courts for playing ball games, and tombs in which finely crafted jewelry has been found. Agriculture using **irrigation** systems was well developed and supplied the city's large population with an abundance of crops. The ancient Zapotec people also had knowledge of mathematics, created a calendar, and had one of the earliest systems of writing in the area. Their writing system is believed to have influenced the alphabets later used by the Aztec and Mayan peoples.

Culture Cues

☼ Mexico has the largest Spanish-speaking population of any country in the world.

☼ The Mexican government officially recognizes 62 indigenous groups and provides protection for their culture and languages. Indigenous peoples make up about 10 percent of the population or a little more than 12.7 million people.

☼ Mexico is the 11th largest country in the world in terms of area. It is the fifth largest country in the Americas.

☼ The capital of Mexico is Mexico City. It is the country's largest city and has a population of more than 8 million. Combined with the surrounding metropolitan areas, Mexico City has a population of more than 21 million.

Stories and Legends

The jaguar represents the Zapotecs' belief that they were transformed from animals.

Like most of the other Mesoamerican peoples, the Zapotecs had many gods. Some were associated with agriculture or fertility. Two of the Zapotecs' most important gods were Cocijo, the god of lightning and rain, and Coquihani, the god of light. The god of maize, or corn, was common in many of the Mesoamerican cultures. The Zapotecs called this god Pitao Cozobi. The Zapotecs may also have recognized gods from other nearby peoples, such as the feathered serpent. This god was known as Quetzalcoatl to the Aztecs, but it had different names in other cultures.

The Zapotecs called themselves "Be'ena'a," meaning "The People" or "The True People" in their language. They believed that they were the original inhabitants of the Valley of Oaxaca.

Cocijo is often represented wearing a ceremonial hat.

The Zapotecs have no legends and stories about their people traveling to the Valley of Oaxaca from somewhere else. They believe that their ancestors emerged from the earth or from caves, or that they were born from rocks. There are also stories about their ancestors being transformed into people from trees or from animals like the jaguar, puma, or ocelot. The Zapotecs believe that they are a people descended from supernatural beings that lived among the clouds. They believe that when they die, they will return to their home in the clouds. In the Central Valley Zapotec language, "The Cloud People" translates as "Be'ena' Za'a." Though many Zapotecs may not believe these stories any longer, they remain an important part of Zapotec culture.

The Zapotecs called on gods like Pitao Cozobi for help with their crops.

THE STORY OF
Coyote and Rabbit

Rabbit was eating out on the plain one day when he met Coyote. "I'm hungry," Coyote told him. "I'm going to eat you."

"Wait and I'll bring you some chicken instead," said Rabbit.

Rabbit ran away. After some time, Coyote grew impatient and followed Rabbit's tracks. He found Rabbit leaning against a cliff. "What are you doing?" Coyote asked.

"I'm holding up the cliff so that it does not fall down," said Rabbit. "Can you hold it up for me?" Rabbit asked. "Then, I can go and get your chicken."

Coyote agreed to help. He leaned against the cliff, and Rabbit ran off. Coyote waited for a long time. Finally, he moved away from the cliff. It did not fall down. Coyote was very angry and left to find Rabbit again.

"Be patient," said Rabbit. "The food will be here soon. I will go and check."

Rabbit ran off but soon stopped. He started a fire around where Coyote was waiting. He went back to Coyote and told him food was on the way.

Rabbit then ran away. Coyote was happy that his chicken was almost ready. Soon, the fire surrounded Coyote. He was never seen again.

The Zapotec civilization began about 500 BC, in what is now the Mexican state of Oaxaca. The main political center was Monte Albán. This was one of the earliest cities in Mesoamerica. After 200 BC, Monte Albán became the center of the Zapotec empire in southern Mexico. The city of Mitla was the main Zapotec religious center. Eventually, the empire declined and Monte Albán and other sites were abandoned. The Zapotecs later came into conflict with the nearby **Mixtecs**, before the Aztecs conquered both peoples by 1502.

When the Spanish arrived in Mesoamerica, they were able to make alliances with some of the native peoples who were opposed to Aztec rule. This helped the Spanish commander **Hernan Cortes** and his soldiers, known as **conquistadores**, to defeat the Aztec empire in 1521. The Zapotecs decided not to resist the Spanish because they did not want to suffer the same fate as the Aztecs. The Spanish still attacked but it took them several years to conquer the Zapotecs. The Zapotecs rebelled against the Spanish conquerors three times, the last time in 1715.

Timeline of the Zapotecs

700–1000 The Zapotec Empire declines, and many sites are abandoned.

1521 Spanish conquistadores conquer the Aztec Empire. It takes several campaigns from 1522 to 1527 before the Spanish forces are able to conquer the Zapotecs.

500–200 BC The city of Monte Albán is established.

250–700 AD The Zapotecs are at the height of their power in southern Mexico.

1000–1500 The Mixtecs take over some Zapotec sites, but there is still warfare between the two groups. Both peoples come into conflict with the Aztec empire further north.

1497–1502 The Aztecs conquer the Zapotec people.

The Spanish established a new empire called the Viceroyalty of **New Spain**. The capital was the old Aztec city of Tenochtitlan, which the Spanish rebuilt as Mexico City. New Spain included large parts of what are now the western United States, Central America, the Caribbean, and Mexico. This included the region occupied by the Zapotecs.

All the Mesoamerican peoples experienced war and forced labor, and had no immunity from European diseases, such as smallpox and measles. It is estimated that these diseases killed more than 90 percent of the indigenous population. The Zapotec population was about 350,000 in the 1520s but dropped to about 40,000 a century later.

Like many of the indigenous Mesoamerican peoples, the Zapotecs adopted the Roman Catholic faith of their Spanish conquerors, adding elements of their own traditional religions. Zapotecs became important members of society after Mexican independence in 1821. They are recognized as a distinct people and their language and culture are legally protected.

1550 and 1560 Zapotec uprisings against the rulers of New Spain are defeated.

1810 Mexico declares independence, which Spain recognizes in 1821 following Mexico's War of Independence.

1910–1920
The Mexican Revolution leads to the Constitution of 1917. This recognizes indigenous people and protects their languages and cultures.

1715 Final Zapotec revolt against Spanish rule.

1824 The state of Oaxaca is founded within the newly established Mexican Republic.

2003 The General Law of Linguistic Rights of Indigenous Peoples recognizes 62 indigenous languages as "national languages" equal to Spanish.

Social Structures

The majority of Zapotecs are farmers. They grow crops for their own families and for trade. They also keep domestic animals. The crops they grow include maize, beans, and various varieties of squash. Other crops may be grown depending on the climate, soil, and water supply in a particular region.

In ancient Zapotec society, women and men were considered equals, with equal social standings. Only after the Spanish arrived did the idea of women being inferior to men become part of the culture. Today, men tend to farm while women tend to take care of the children and the household. Many women are also expected to work outside the home to help support the family financially, especially in poorer Zapotec communities. Istmeno Zapotec women are well known as traders in their marketplaces. Sometimes, men in the community are not allowed to take on this role. In other regions, however, both men and women produce and sell various goods.

Zapotec handcrafted rugs, blankets, and other woven items are sold in outdoor markets. Items are sold to tourists and locals alike.

In some Zapotec communities, men are well-known and respected artists who create masterpieces of woven material.

Some Zapotec men are highly skilled weavers. Families pass on their weaving techniques from generation to generation. The Zapotec men sell their woven goods at village shops and markets, and some of their work ends up in galleries and stores in the southwestern United States.

The Seasons

The Zapotec people live in many different areas. They experience different climates, depending on where they live. At the higher elevations of the Oaxaca valley, there is a mild climate. The coastal regions are tropical. All the regions the Zapotecs live in have dry and rainy seasons. The rainy season is from May to October.

Communication

The ancient Zapotecs developed one of the earliest systems of writing in Mesoamerica. The Zapotec system is believed to have influenced the alphabets later used by the Mayan and Aztec cultures. There is no one single Zapotec language. Zapotec languages belong to the **Otomanguean** Language Family, a group of closely related Mesoamerican languages. It is believed that the language first developed about 1500 BC and later split into different branches, including the Zapotec languages. Today, the Zapotec of Oaxaca still speak these ancient languages.

The Zapotec languages are tonal. This means that the meaning of a word is often determined by the tone and pitch of the speaker's voice. These tones are called **tonemes**. They consist of high, low, rising, and falling voice pitches. There are many different Zapotec **dialects**.

Zapotec people continue to speak in traditional Zapotec languages, although most also speak Spanish.

The most widely used Zapotec language is Isthmus Zapotec. It is spoken mainly by people living on the Pacific coast of Oaxaca. There are currently about half a million people familiar with this dialect, with a few in nearby states. Isthmus Zapotec language programming can be heard on local radio stations.

Although the Isthmus Zapotec language is the most common, there are thought to be at least nine separate Zapotec languages. The number of speakers of these languages varies. Experts estimate that more than 70,000 people speak Loxicha Zapotec, while only a small fraction of people speak San Felipe Tejalapan Zapotec. Few people speak San Agustin Mixtepec Zapotec today, and the language may become extinct.

Ancient Zapotec people developed a written form of language using a variety of images and symbols.

Speaking Zapotec

The difference in Zapotec languages can be very great, even between two villages that are close to one another. Though the words are often different, the way the different Zapotec languages are spoken is similar. First, the Zapotec say the verb. Then they say the subject of the sentence. In Zapotec languages, a sentence such as "Mary kicks the ball" would be "kicks Mary ball."

Some Zapotec words have apostrophes. This means there should be a pause. This pause is like the one English speakers use when saying "uh-oh." Scientists are beginning to study Zapotec languages more. They want to make sure Zapotec languages do not disappear.

In Isthmus Zapotec, "Hello, my name is …" is spoken as "Pa diuxi, nea liah …"

Law and Order

Before 1994, land in Mexico, including the Zapotec region, was either communal, private, or ejidos. Communal land is owned by community members and governed by local authorities. This type of land usually is of poor quality for growing crops. Private land includes separate parcels owned by different people.

Ejidos, which are often located in aboriginal villages, are owned and operated by individuals or groups of village residents. They can comprise small portions of land in and around the village or sometimes include the entire community. While corporations now own some ejidos, most are still owned by farmers. Today, ejidos make up more than half of Mexico's farmland.

In most Zapotec communities, citizens are elected to local government or church positions in what is known as a cargo system. Under this system, men serve terms of office without payment. Positions include judges, mayors, police officials, and treasurers. Men usually serve for one year and can alternate between church and local government roles. Men are given greater responsibility as they get older. Local authorities examine disputes between individuals in the community. These authorities have the power to fine and even imprison offenders if necessary.

Oaxaca is divided into eight main regions and hundreds of small villages. The government of Oaxaca include a governor as well as legislative and judicial branches.

Some Zapotec farmers still use oxen rather than modern machinery to help plow their farmland.

Local Mexican government buildings often feature displays for important holidays, such as Day of the Dead.

Celebrating Culture

During festivals, Zapotecs perform a variety of unique dances, such as the pineapple dance.

The ancient Zapotecs believed in gods associated with the weather, such as rain and lightning storms. Today, most Zapotecs are Roman Catholic, and patron saints are very important in their communities. Ancient religious beliefs have been combined with the Zapotecs' Catholic beliefs.

Annual celebrations take place in Zapotec communities all over Oaxaca. These include the fiestas, or festivals, of local patron saints. Some locations have very large and elaborate events, such as the festival of El Rosario in Teotitlan del Valle. In San Pedro Amuzgos, there are celebrations for the day of Saint Peter. At San Andres Huaxpaltepec, on the Pacific coast, the Zapotecs commemorate the day of Jesus the Nazarene.

Each festival includes special parties, wide varieties of food, thousands of flowers, and many different activities. In addition to the colorful religious processions and traditional church ceremonies, communities host popular dances, parades, and sporting events. In some areas, there might be brass bands, bullfights, beauty pageants, feasts, large-scale firework displays, and open-air markets. Artisans often travel great distances to attend these celebrations. They often set up stalls for their handicrafts on the local streets or in public parks. There may also be plays and other public shows featuring costumed actors, musicians, and other performers.

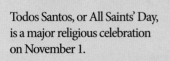
Todos Santos, or All Saints' Day, is a major religious celebration on November 1.

Art and Culture

The architecture and artwork of the ancient Zapotecs can be seen in the temples, compounds, and other buildings in Monte Albán and Mitla. **Archaeologists** have also found finely crafted Zapotec jewelry at other sites in Mexico. The finest examples of culture and art can be found at Mitla, the Zapotec religious center.

The word *Mitla* means "place of the dead and the underworld." Intricate mosaics cover tombs, panels, and entire walls in many of Mitla's buildings. These mosaics are made of many small, finely cut and polished stone pieces. These pieces are fitted together without mortar. The stones are kept in place by the weight of adjacent pieces wedged against them. In ancient times, the mosaics were set against a red painted background.

Ancient Zapotec structures in Monte Albán include pyramids, terraces, and large stone staircases carved with life-sized figures. These figures are thought to represent prisoners captured after battles. One building has more than 40 stones carved with **hieroglyphic** writing and images of heads wearing headdresses.

Traditional Zapotec mosaic art is used to create religious artifacts and relics.

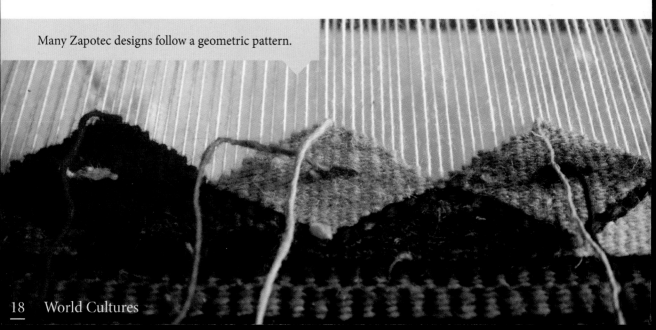

Many Zapotec designs follow a geometric pattern.

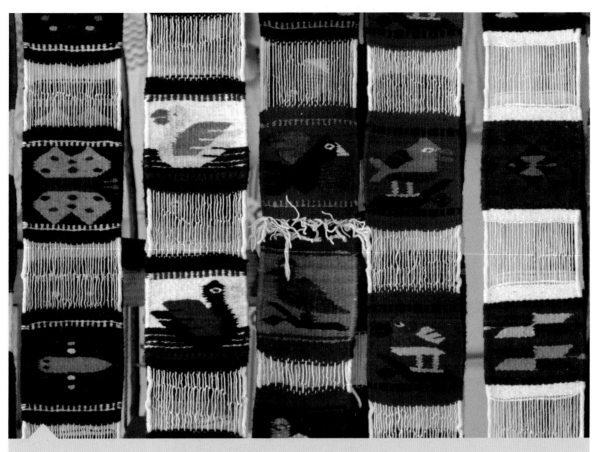

Zapotec weavers incorporate birds, butterflies, flowers, and other symbols in their work.

Archaeologists believe these may represent other territories conquered by the Zapotecs. Tombs containing urns, statues, and funeral effigies of gods and animals, such as eagles and jaguars, can also be found there. The ancient Zapotecs also made very distinctive pottery.

Today, Zapotec towns are renowned for their weaving, pottery, and other handicrafts. The weaving for heavier items such as blankets, rugs, and ponchos is done on horizontal looms. Traditional clothing is usually woven on backstrap looms, a traditional kind of loom used by the ancient Zapotecs. The weavers use a combination of Zapotec and other designs.

Culture

Alebrijes are wooden carvings of real or imaginary creatures. The Zapotecs used to make the Alebrijes from papier-mache or cardboard. Today, they are often made of wood. The Zapotecs use knives and chisels to create the alebrijes. In the past, the figures were decorated with dyes made from local plants, insects, and minerals. Today, artists mostly use paints on their creations. Alebrijes are very popular with tourists.

Dressing Up

The clothes and decoration worn by the ancient Zapotecs usually indicated a person's social status, profession, and place of origin. Most clothing was made of cotton.

Men wore a loincloth with long flaps at the front and back. Most men did not wear shirts, but some wore sleeveless cotton tunics. Other pieces of clothing included cotton headbands and white cloaks that were tied at one shoulder. Nobles, priests, and soldiers wore sandals, but most people were barefoot. Warrior headdresses were very decorative and made from leather and wood. They were often adorned with the feathers of eagles and colorful birds called quetzals. Red and white were frequently used colors in warrior clothing. Women wore long skirts and huipils. Huipils are tops that resemble ponchos decorated with strips of colored yarn. The type of huipil worn indicated a woman's marital status, as well as her social status.

People can often identify a Zapotec woman's village from her style of dress.

Traditional Zapotec clothing includes bright colors and vivid patterns. Women often wear an array of colorful ribbons in their hair.

Today, Zapotec people wear both traditional and modern clothing. Women's traditional dress consists of embroidered blouses and more Western-style blouses on top. The long wrap skirt is often made of plaid fabric, and there is an underskirt or slip. A bib apron may be worn with the costume, along with a woven sash called a cenidor. Women wearing traditional costumes usually have their hair in braids. In some villages, women use rectangular garments called rebozos as scarves or headwraps. The style of rebozos varies from region to region.

Most men wear modern clothing. Traditional wear includes a loose shirt with wide, loose pants, sandals, and a straw or wool hat. Older men may still wear traditional hats with modern clothing.

Jewelry

Archaeologists have found many fine examples of jewelry made by the ancient Zapotecs. These ancient Zapotec artists often decorated their jewelry with religious symbols and figures. After the Spanish conquest, jewelry featuring Christian symbols became more common. Today, Zapotec jewelers in Oaxaca produce handcrafted items in traditional designs.

Food and Fun

Oaxaca is well known for its seven moles, or sauces. The Zapotecs toast and grind a variety of chili peppers, seeds, herbs, and spices to create and flavor the moles. Chocolate is used to make some moles and is often served as a drink. The drink is made with cacao beans, which are the dried, cured seeds of the cacao fruit. The beans are ground, then combined with almonds, cinnamon, and sugar into bars. Pieces are mixed with hot milk or water for drinking.

The food of the ancient Zapotecs included corn, tomatoes, squashes, beans, chili peppers, and cacao. Cacao beans were considered very valuable and were even used as currency in some ancient Mesoamerican cultures. People in cacao growing areas often paid their taxes with cacao beans. After the Spanish arrived, they sent chocolate to Europe. At first, it was used as a beverage. Europeans replaced the chili pepper in the drink with sugar, and chocolate became a popular drink with the upper classes. By the early nineteenth century, chocolate was being made into the bars we are familiar with today.

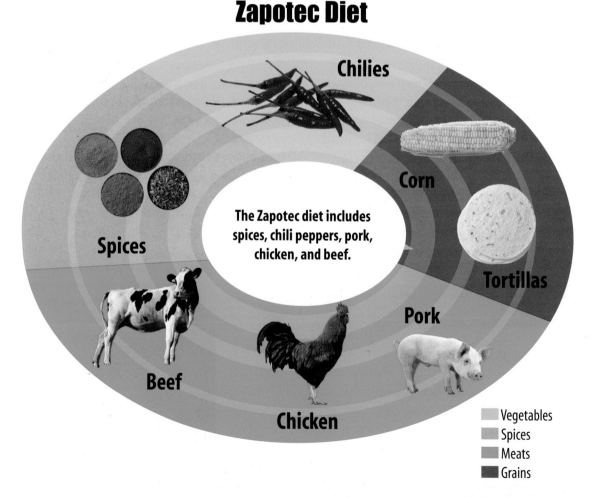

Zapotec Diet

Chilies

Corn

Tortillas

Spices

The Zapotec diet includes spices, chili peppers, pork, chicken, and beef.

Pork

Beef

Chicken

- Vegetables
- Spices
- Meats
- Grains

The Spanish conquest brought new ingredients such as cinnamon, cumin, and cloves, as well as meat from cattle, chicken, and pigs. The Spanish also introduced baking and frying. This added to the dry roasting and steaming practiced by the native peoples.

Popcorn was part of life for the Mesoamerican peoples, including the Zapotecs, long before it was introduced to the rest of the world at the time of the Spanish conquest. Popcorn was used to decorate ceremonial headdresses and necklaces. It was also used as an ornament on statues of gods. An early Spanish account spoke of a Mesoamerican ceremony involving "a kind of corn that bursts when parched and discloses its contents and makes itself look like a very white flower."

Traditional Zapotec food is prepared on corn tortillas. Moles and other sauces are used to top the tortillas.

Zapotecs use the corn dough known as masa to make tamales and different types of tortillas. Gordas and blandas are thick tortillas. Clayudas are huge, dense, and flat, and empanadas are stuffed tortilla pies. Zapotec cheeses include firm Queso Anejo, crumbly Queso Fresco, and a cheese similar to mozzarella that is shaped like a ball.

Grasshoppers and Worms

Chapulines are a type of grasshopper that is fried, seasoned with salt, lime, and chili pepper, and then served as an appetizer. Another unusual menu item is gusanitos de maguey, or maguey worms. They are not really worms, but the larvae of an insect that lives on the maguey plant. Gusanitos are smoked and then added to salsas and other dishes as flavoring.

Great Ideas

Soccer, baseball, and basketball are popular in Oaxaca today. In ancient times, the Zapotec played different types of Mesoamerican ball games in different regions. A modern version of these games, called ulama, is still played in northwestern Mexico.

The exact rules of the ancient games are unknown, but the games may have been similar to volleyball without a net. Players had to keep the ball in play. They scored points when the ball was not returned or went out of the court.

In some areas, stone goals were fixed high on the sides of the ball courts. It might have been difficult to get the ball through these goals.

Players usually struck the ball with their hips, although in some versions of the game they used their forearms, bats, or rackets. The ball could weigh as much as 9 pounds (4 kilograms) and was made of solid rubber. The heavy ball could sometimes cause severe injuries.

Sometimes, rival groups played ball games instead of going to battle with each other. These games were large, formal events. Women and children also played the sport for recreation on homemade courts.

Ancient Zapotec ball courts were long and narrow, with walls along the sides against which the ball could bounce.

Rubber

Today, many familiar products are made from rubber, including tires, water hoses, and shoe soles. The process used to make modern rubber was invented in the 19th century. However, the ancient peoples of Mesoamerica were using rubber as early as 1500 BC. Milky fluid called latex was extracted from local rubber trees and mixed with juice from plant vines to create processed rubber. When the Spanish arrived, rubber was being used for many things by the native peoples, including balls for the local ball game.

At Issue

Oaxaca is one of the poorest parts of Mexico. Its culture has remained mostly agricultural since Mexico became independent in 1821. The state has some of the nation's highest rates of illiteracy, infant mortality, and malnutrition. This is especially true among the indigenous populations, including the Zapotecs.

Land reforms by the Mexican government have led to indigenous peoples losing many of their traditional lands. Many Zapotecs are farmers and depend on agriculture for their livelihood. As the oil industry has developed, Zapotecs have concerns about pollution and damage to their farmland. There are demands for greater investment by the Mexican government in local social services, such as health and education. Infrastructure, such as roads, bridges, electricity power lines, and fresh water supplies, is also important.

The Zapotec people would also like more control over their own affairs in local government. There has been social unrest, such as the teacher's strike of 2006, which was supported by groups protesting against government corruption and social injustice. There have also been armed revolts in the neighboring state of Chiapas, leading to the deployment of the Mexican army in the area.

The ancient city of Monte Albán is a popular tourist destination. However, the site is threatened by urban growth in the surrounding area. Four different local governments control the archaeological remains. This makes it difficult to coordinate efforts to control urban growth and protect the site.

Tourists from around the world visit Monte Albán. They come to learn about the rich history of the ancient Zapotecs and to experience Zapotec culture today.

Into the Future

The Mexican Constitution recognizes indigenous peoples and protects their languages and cultures. However, Zapotecs and other indigenous peoples continue to face problems.

Only 34 percent of people living in Mexico's indigenous regions have health insurance and access to health care facilities. In other parts of the country, 47 percent of the population has health insurance and access to hospitals and clinics. General standards of health are very low in the Zapotec community. Sanitation and education standards are also below those of Mexico's other indigenous regions. While work is being done to raise standards and improve the lives of the Zapotec people, this will take time. Poor economic conditions and high unemployment rates continue to cause people to migrate in search of work, either to other parts of Mexico or to the United States.

For many years, Zapotecs were treated unfairly in the justice system. Only the Spanish language was used, making it difficult for speakers of other languages to understand and communicate. In 2003, the General Law of Linguistic Rights of Indigenous Peoples recognized 62 indigenous languages as national languages. Those languages are now equal to Spanish in all territories. This means that indigenous peoples can use their native language to communicate with their government.

The Mexican Constitution, signed in 1917, protects the rights of the Mexican people.

Role-play Debate

W hen people debate a topic, two sides take a different viewpoint about one idea. Each side presents logical arguments to support its views. In a role-play debate, participants act out the roles of the key people or groups involved with the different viewpoints. Role-playing can build communication skills and help people understand how others may think and feel. Usually, each person or team is given a set amount of time to present its case. The participants take turns stating their arguments until the time set aside for the debate is up.

THE ISSUE

The Mexican constitution recognizes the rights of indigenous peoples, such as the Zapotecs, and protects their language and culture. However, each Mexican state can also make its own laws, and the rights of native peoples may not be protected as well as they should be in some areas. Many Zapotecs feel that they should have more control over their own affairs, including local government, health care, education, justice, land ownership, and the management of natural resources.

THE QUESTION

Should the Zapotecs be given greater control over local government and their own affairs, including ownership of natural resources?

THE SIDES

NO

Government: Current laws do a good job of protecting Zapotec communities. Reforms can be made where differences exist between federal and state governments. The Mexican government will always make sure that the Zapotecs' quality of life and natural resources are preserved.

YES

Zapotecs: The government has not been able to fully enforce the laws that protect the Zapotecs and their culture. State governments often make their own laws and sometimes discriminate against the Zapotecs. The Zapotecs should be able to control their own affairs, including their land's natural resources.

Ready, Set, Go

Form two teams to debate the issue, and decide whether your team will play the role of the government or the role of Zapotecs. Each team should take time to use this book and other research to develop solid arguments for its side and to understand how the issue affects each group. At the end of the role-play debate, discuss how you feel after hearing both points of view.

World Cultures Quiz!

1 What was the main city of the Zapotec empire?

2 How many indigenous groups does the Mexican government officially recognize?

3 Who was the Spanish leader of the conquistadores in 1521?

4 The Zapotec languages are part of what group?

5 In what state do most of the Zapotec people live?

6 What modern game is based on the ancient Mesoamerican ball game?

7 When was the last Zapotec rebellion against the Spanish?

8 What does the Zapotec phrase Be'ena' Za'a mean in English?

9 What are chapulines?

10 What bean did the ancient Mesoamerican peoples use to make a hot chocolate drink?

Key Words

archaeologist: a scientist who studies the human past

Aztecs: an indigenous Mesoamerican culture conquered by the Spanish in 1521

conquistadores: Spanish soldiers and adventurers who took part in the conquest of Mexico and Peru in the sixteenth century

dialect a form of language spoken in a certain area

hieroglyphic: an ancient type of writing using picture symbols

Hernan Cortes: leader of the Spanish forces that conquered the Aztec empire

indigenous: originally from a particular region or country

irrigation: supplying dry land with water by means of artificial channels and ditches

isthmus: a thin strip of land that connects two larger pieces of land

Mayans: an indigenous people who also had an ancient culture in Yucatan, Belize, and Guatemala

Mixtecs: an indigenous people in the state of Oaxaca in Mexico

New Spain: the name of the Spanish-ruled areas of Mexico and other parts of the Americas that were established in 1535

Otomanguean: an ancient family of closely related Mesoamerican languages, including those of the Zapotec

tonemes: vocal sounds that express the meaning of a word

Index

Log on to www.av2books.com

AV² by Weigl brings you media enhanced books that support active learning. Go to www.av2books.com, and enter the special code found on page 2 of this book. You will gain access to enriched and enhanced content that supplements and complements this book. Content includes video, audio, weblinks, quizzes, a slide show, and activities.

AV² Online Navigation

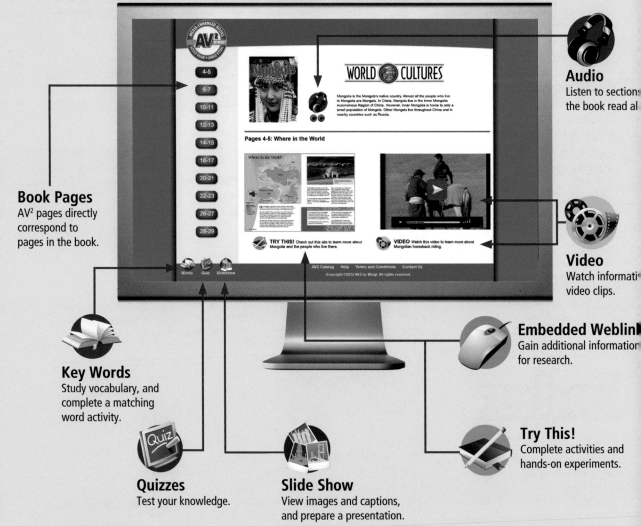

Audio
Listen to sections the book read al

Video
Watch informati video clips.

Embedded Weblin
Gain additional information for research.

Try This!
Complete activities and hands-on experiments.

Book Pages
AV² pages directly correspond to pages in the book.

Key Words
Study vocabulary, and complete a matching word activity.

Quizzes
Test your knowledge.

Slide Show
View images and captions, and prepare a presentation.

AV² was built to bridge the gap between print and digital. We encourage you to tell us what you like and what you want to see in the future.

Sign up to be an AV² Ambassador at www.av2books.com/ambassador.